D0819851

FORESTRY

Heather Kissock

Weigl

www.weigl.com

Published by Weigl Educational Publishers Limited
6325 – 10 Street SE
Calgary, Alberta, Canada
T2H 2Z9
Web site: www.weigl.ca

Library and Archives Canada Cataloguing in Publication

Kissock, Heather
Forestry / Heather Kissock.

(Canadian industries)
Includes index.
ISBN 1-55388-228-8 (bound)
ISBN 1-55388-229-6 (pbk.)

1. Forests and forestry--Canada--Juvenile literature. 2. Forests and
forestry--Economic aspects--Canada--Juvenile literature. 3. Forests and
forestry--Canada--History--Juvenile literature. I. Title. II. Series:
Canadian industries (Calgary, Alta.)

SD145.K57 2007   j634.90971   C2006-902499-5

Printed in Canada
1 2 3 4 5 6 7 8 9 0   10 09 08 07 06

Project Coordinator: Heather Kissock
Designer: Warren Clark

We gratefully acknowledge the financial support of the Government of Canada through the Book Publishing
Industry Development Program (BPIDP) for our publishing activities.

Canadian Forestry Association (Elzabeth Muckle-Jeffs): page 11.

Consultants: Allistar Hain and Chris Lee of the Canadian Forest Service (Natural Resources Canada)

Contents

Overview 4

Forestry in Canada 6

Canada's Forests 8

Canada's Forestry Beginnings 10

Forestry Then and Now 12

Softwood Lumber 14

Wood Pulp 16

Careers in Forestry 18

Facing the Issues 20

Canadian Forestry in the World 22

Forests Around the World 24

Charting the World's Forests 26

Supplying the Demand 28

From Canada to the World 30

Forestry Technology 32

Forestry's Impact on Canadians 34

Helping Others 36

Looking to the Future 38

Timeline of Forestry Events 40

Research Activity 42

Forestry Experiment 43

What Do You Know? 45

Further Research 46

Glossary 47

Index 48

Overview

From its land to its people, Canada is a diverse country. This diversity lends itself to a range of industries. Major industries in Canada include agriculture, energy, fishing, forestry, mining, and **manufacturing**. Each of these industries require people with various skills. As a result, Canadians can work in almost any field they like without leaving the country. People from other countries view Canada as a land of opportunity as well. Many come to Canada to find work, to create businesses, or to otherwise contribute to the economic landscape.

Canada's industries have global impact. The country's natural resources are shipped both raw and as manufactured products to many parts of the world. Sometimes, they are sold to other countries. On other occasions, they are sent for humanitarian

Agriculture

Agriculture, or farming, is an industry that uses the land to grow crops and raise animals for food and other products. Canadian crops include grains, such as wheat, barley, and canola, as well as fruits and vegetables. Cattle, sheep, and swine are just some of the animals raised on Canada's farms.

Energy

Energy provides the electricity that lights rooms, the gas that makes cars and trucks run, and the oil that heats buildings. It comes from natural resources such as water, natural gas, petroleum, coal, and uranium. Due to the abundance of these resources, Canada is a world leader in energy production.

Fishing

With 202,080 kilometres of coastline, Canada has access to more fish and shellfish than most other countries. Salmon, cod, and sole are just some of the fish caught off Canada's coasts. Shellfish caught in Canada's waters include lobster and shrimp. Fish farms, in which fish are raised and harvested like farm animals, also contribute to the fishing industry in Canada.

purposes, in order to help countries that have an urgent need for materials. Canadian products are known worldwide for their quality. In order to maintain and improve this quality, Canadians are constantly developing and implementing new technologies and methods, all the while keeping an eye on the impact these technologies have on people and the environment.

Canadians can work in almost any field they like without leaving the country.

Forestry

Forests cover about 40 percent of Canada's land surface, and approximately 245 million hectares of these forests are timber-productive. This means that the trees in these areas can be used to manufacture other products. Spruce, pine, cedar, and fir are all timber-productive trees found in Canada's forests.

Mining

Minerals of all kinds are found deep inside Canada's land. These minerals have a range of uses. Once it is mined from the ground, Canada's zinc is used in sunscreen. Its sand and gravel are used to build houses and roads. Its gold and diamonds are used to make jewelry. Other minerals mined in Canada include copper, potash, and nickel.

Manufacturing

Canada uses its natural resources to create a variety of products. At pulp and paper mills, trees are used to make paper. Nickel is used to create stainless steel for eating utensils. Besides sunscreen, zinc is also used to create the galvanized steel used in the construction of buildings, aircraft parts, and telecommunication equipment.

Forestry in Canada

Canada is a land of trees. Approximately 310 million hectares, or 31 percent of Canada's total area, is forested. Canada possesses many tree species, including spruce, pine, fir, and aspen, that are used to make a variety of products. It is no wonder that Canada is the world's premier exporter of forest products.

The country's forestry industry had more modest beginnings, however. Initially, the forests were used on an "as needed" basis by Canada's Aboriginal peoples. The forests provided the animals, plants, and wood that these people needed to survive. The arrival of the Europeans changed the way Canada's forests were used. Trees were cut down and sold to businesses and organizations for profit. Canada's forestry industry was born, and eventually it became a major supplier of **softwood lumber** and **wood pulp**.

When the industry was in its infancy, little regard was paid to the number of trees being cut down. Over time, however, people became aware that forests provided more than just wood. Their role in **cultural** and social activities began to be

Our model forests now serve as the prototype for sustainable forestry in many parts of the world.

■ Riparian zones are the areas of vegetation growing along the edges of bodies of water, such as the Adams River in British Columbia. Preserving riparian areas is very important because they prevent soil erosion, provide shelter for animals, and keep water clean.

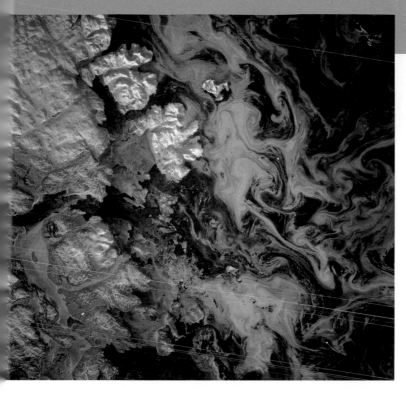

Satellite photographs show Canada's unique landscape, including forests.

recognized. Forests began to be viewed as integral parts of the Canadian community. The industry was challenged to find ways to balance the needs of the industry with the needs of the country's citizens.

The development of the model forest has been the industry's response to this challenge. Canada's model forests lead the way in researching and developing cutting-edge techniques in **sustainable** forest management. Our model forests now serve as the prototype for sustainable forestry in many parts of the world.

Still, sustainability has not been the only issue facing Canada's forest industry. Since the early 1990s, Canada and the United States were in disagreement over the softwood lumber **trade**, with the United States limiting the amount of lumber that could come into their country. Canada considered that these actions were in violation of the **free trade agreement** between the two countries. The United States is Canada's largest customer of wood and wood products, and strict **tariffs** were

placed on Canadian softwood shipments into the United States in 2001 to protect the American lumber industry.

In May 2006, a new agreement was reached between the United States and Canadian governments that lifted these tariffs. Now Canada can export up to 34 percent of the United States softwood lumber market before any taxes are imposed. This helps maintain prices and protect the softwood producers in both countries.

Nature also creates its own problems for the forest. Insects, such as the mountain pine beetle, can infest and ruin large tracts of forest, impacting heavily on the industry's **economy**. Forest fires can also destroy large sections of forested land. Like all living things, trees can also fall victim to diseases that make them worthless in the marketplace.

Science and technology, however, are doing much to control and monitor issues relating to fire, insects, disease, and sustainability. Satellites and aerial photography are just two ways in which technology is being used to protect Canada's forests and keep them viable for years to come.

BUSINESS BITS

Canada has 10 percent of the world's forests.

Canada's forestry industry generates about $80 billion every year.

About 93,000 plants, animals, and microorganisms live in Canada's forests.

Only 119 million hectares, or 28 percent of Canada's forested land, is currently used for timber production.

Canada's Forests

Of Canada's 310 million hectares of forest, 293 million hectares are available for **commercial** use. This means that these parts of the forest can be logged for wood and wood products. The remainder of the forested land has been set aside for parks, **conservation** projects, or private use. Canada harvests about 0.4 percent of its commercial forests every year. Most of this wood is used to make lumber, plywood, and wood pulp for paper production. This map shows Canada's **boreal** region. Canada's boreal forests are located within this region.

THINK ABOUT IT ▼

What role do trees play in your life? Take a look around your home, classroom, and neighbourhood. How many objects are made from wood? How often do you use these things?

Boreal Cordillera ⬛

Taiga Cordillera ⬛

Boreal Plains ⬜

Taiga Shield ⬛

Boreal Shield ⬛

Atlantic Maritime ⬛

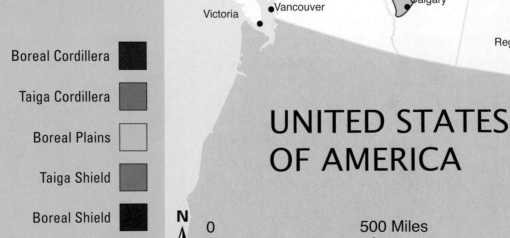

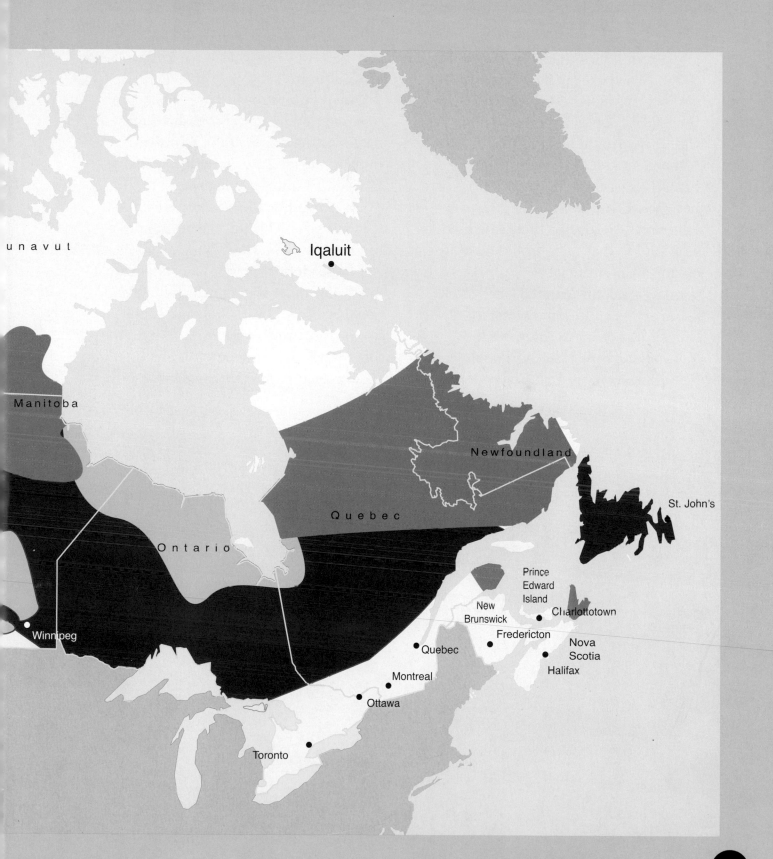

Canada's Forestry Beginnings

As with most nations, forestry in Canada began as a means of survival. Forests provided Aboriginal Peoples with plants and wildlife that could be used for food, clothing, and medicines. The trees themselves were cut down and used as fuel, shelter, and transportation. Sometimes, controlled fires were used to clear land so that there would be more grazing area for the larger animals the Aboriginal Peoples hunted, such as elk, bison, and deer. In some cases, forests were cleared to make room for the planting of crops. The Aboriginal Peoples viewed the forest as a natural provider, and, because of this, a source of **spirituality**.

When Europeans first arrived and began to explore, they too realized that the forests held a wealth of resources. Initially, the forests were seen as a source of wildlife. Animals living within the forests, including the beaver, were hunted for their pelts. This was the beginning of the fur trade in Canada.

Forests dominated the land, and people looked for other ways in which the trees could be used. The 1600s heralded the beginning of industrial forestry. Trees were logged to supply timber to the shipbuilding industries in both France and Great Britain.

■ French and British settlers began the commercial logging industry in what is now Canada.

As time went on, Canada's forestry industry expanded. By the late 1800s, Canada was supplying trees for the pulp and paper industry as well.

Timber was in demand, and the young country appeared to have an inexhaustible supply. Trees were cut down in order to meet this demand without much consideration for future needs. Over time, however, people began to realize that Canada's forests had a limited number of trees, and if the forestry industry were to remain productive, these supplies had to be managed better. Forestry experts began practicing sustained yield forestry in an effort to keep Canada's tree levels high. They did this by promoting the idea of planting trees in areas that had been stripped bare. This included land that had been logged for timber or cleared for agriculture.

In the late 1900s, people began to realize that forests provided more than just timber. They contained unique plants and animals that required forest cover to survive. They also provided people with opportunities for social and cultural activities. As a result of these changing views, the Canadian forestry industry began to move toward sustainable forestry practices. This approach attempts to balance timber production with the needs of the people, plants, and wildlife that live in and near forested areas.

In 1992, representatives from Canada's federal, territorial, and provincial governments signed the Canada Forest Accord. The goal of this agreement was to ensure the long-term health of Canada's forest ecosystem so that it could continue to be available for environmental, economic, social, and cultural use. These goals were to be achieved through the National Forest Strategy, a plan of action that protected at-risk forests, regulated the size of timber harvests, banned harmful pesticides, and encourages cooperation between all forests **stakeholders**. This program set the groundwork for sustainable practices in Canadian forestry.

> Timber was in demand, and the young country appeared to have an inexhaustible supply.

Elihu Stewart

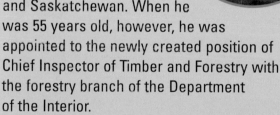

Elihu Stewart is known as the man who spearheaded forest conservation in Canada. Born in Collingwood, Ontario, in 1844, Stewart spent most of his adult years as a land surveyor, working in both Ontario and Saskatchewan. When he was 55 years old, however, he was appointed to the newly created position of Chief Inspector of Timber and Forestry with the forestry branch of the Department of the Interior.

As chief inspector, Stewart championed both the conservation and propagation of Canada's forests. He actively promoted the need for forestry education programs in Canada. Stewart was instrumental in developing a reforestation program in western Canada that saw more than 8 million seedlings planted.

Stewart's concern for the conservation of Canada's forests led him to create the Canadian Forestry Association in 1900. The association survives to this day and still promotes the protection and conservation of Canada's forested areas.

Forestry Then and Now

Cutting down trees has always been considered strenuous work. In the early days of Canadian forestry, logging was done mainly with the use of simple tools and animals. Over time, a combination of technology and creativity has helped ease the workload.

THEN

THEN

Felling the Trees

When cutting down trees, the saw is the tool of choice. In the early years of Canadian forestry, sawing trees was time-consuming, manual labour. Saws required two people, one at each end, who worked in tandem, pushing the saw back and forth through the tree until it was loose enough to fall. Most forestry workers now use chainsaws to fell trees. These saws are motor-operated and require only one person to guide the blade through the tree. With the pull of a ripcord, the saw is started. A chain encircling the rim of the blade rotates the blade at high speed, allowing its teeth to cut through the tree.

Hauling Logs in the Forest

Hauling logs through the forest used to be the job of animals, usually oxen or horses. The logs were tied onto a cart that the animals pulled along. Today, a machine called a skidder does the job of hauling logs through the forest. Skidders are large vehicles that are equipped with a cable. The cable is hooked into felled trees, and the skidder then drags them along. Some skidders have a claw-like extension, called a grapple, instead of a cable. The grapple can grab several logs at a time, making the job of hauling more efficient and less time-consuming.

NOW

NOW

THEN

THEN

Hauling the Logs in Mountains

Carting logs from a mountainous area to a loading dock presents a few challenges. Getting the heavy machinery that could be used to gather and carry logs into the mountains can be awkward and impractical. In the early days of Canadian forestry, trees that were felled in mountains were left to roll down to the base. They were then gathered and sent to the mill. Today, these logs are transferred from the mountain using cables. Anchored to tall trees or high steel poles, these cables run along the top of the forest. The logs are attached to the cable and travel over the forest until they reach the loading area, where they are readied to send to the mill.

Transporting the Logs to the Mill

Logs can be transported to the mill by water or by land. When travelling by water, the logs floated with the water current until they reached the mill. This method is still used in some parts of the country. However, when space allows, the logs are often chained into rafts and pulled to the mill by a tugboat. Logs that were travelling to the mill by land were taken by animals initially, but in later years, they were loaded onto railway trains for transport. Trains are still used today, but for the most part, large logging trucks are used to transport the logs from the forest to the mill.

NOW

NOW

13

Softwood Lumber

The majority of Canada's forests consist of softwood trees, such as pine, spruce, and fir, so it is no wonder that Canada's softwood lumber industry is profitable. In a single year, Canada can produce more than 75 million cubic metres of softwood lumber. Only 20 percent of this lumber will be sold in Canada. The rest is sold to the international market. In 2004, softwood lumber was the top forest product export, accounting for 25 percent of all forest products sent from the country.

Lumber is a "first-stage" wood product. It is called this because lumber is only one step away from timber, or the raw wood

Softwoods are popular lumber choices because they are easy to work with.

product. When trees are first cut down, the timber is cut into logs and sent to a sawmill. After stripping the bark from the logs, the timber is cut into boards called lumber. At this point, the lumber is ready to go to market, where it will be used to create "second-stage" wood products, such as doors and windows.

Softwoods are popular lumber choices because they are easy to work with. They are softer than hardwoods, such as birch and maple. Softwood lumber is used primarily in construction. Housing frames are often made from softwood. It is also used in the production of furniture, paneling, and flooring.

Many houses are constructed using softwood lumber and furnished with furniture made from softwood.

Profile

Pamela Perreault

Canada's softwood lumber is a valuable resource. In 2005, the U.S. imported 21.5 billion board feet of softwood lumber from Canada.

Canada's forestry industry provides an estimated 280,000 jobs. However, forests are not just sources of lumber. Forests also have environmental and cultural significance and are important to many people.

Culturally modified trees are found in the rain forests of British Columbia. These trees are important parts of Canadian history and are culturally significant for some Aboriginal groups. The government and forestry industry are working together to preserve these cultural artifacts.

Pamela Perreault has studied culturally modified trees and researches the relationship between Aboriginal peoples and the forestry industry. She has written that culturally modified trees are important indicators of past forest use. Although these trees are protected during forest development planning, Perreault has indicated that perhaps the sites surrounding culturally

■ Sawmills produce lumber that is sold to consumers for a variety of purposes.

> " The government and forestry industry are working together to preserve these cultural artifacts. "

modified trees should have more protection.

Perreault is active in many different organizations. She has been a member at large for the Centre for Native Policy and Research.

As a Ph.D student at the University of British Columbia, Perreault, who is Ojibwa, helped develop a forestry camp for Aboriginal youth. The camp introduces participants to different natural resource professions.

Perreault would like to encourage more Aboriginal youth to become professional foresters or resource managers.

Wood Pulp

Two-thirds of all the trees cut down in Canada each year are turned into wood pulp, most of which is eventually made into paper. Canada has more than 155 pulp and paper mills. They are located mainly in remote areas, close to the forests from which they get their materials. Canada uses much of its wood pulp domestically, but some is still exported to other countries. In 2004, Canada produced about 26 million tonnes of wood pulp. Exports accounted for about 11 million tonnes. The rest was kept and used within Canada.

In 2004, Canada produced about 26 million tonnes of wood pulp.

Most wood pulp comes from waste materials left over from lumber making. When wood is cut into boards of lumber, some smaller pieces remain. These pieces are chopped into small wood chips. The chips are then broken down further using a combination of steam and chemicals. What is left is a porridge of wood and fibre called wood pulp.

Wood pulp can be used to make a variety of paper products. Cardboard boxes and containers originate from wood pulp, as do brown paper bags, newsprint, and writing paper. Even toilet paper starts out as wood pulp. To get to this point, the wood pulp goes through more processing and is treated with more chemicals.

It is this heavy use of chemicals that often brings bad publicity to the wood pulp industry. During the processing of the wood pulp, chemicals are released into the air and water, resulting in environmental pollution. The industry is very aware of the impact these chemicals have on the environment and works closely with scientists and environmental groups to limit the amount of chemicals used and released.

■ Wood chips can also be called wood residue or woodwaste. Woodwaste can be harmful to the environment. The Environmental Protection Act monitors the production of woodwaste and encourages re-use when possible.

Profile

Yonghao Ni

The pulp and paper industry in Canada is important to many communities. There are about 660 pulp and paper mills across Canada, employing more than 80,000 people.

Only the United States produces more pulp and paper products than Canada. The Canadian pulp and paper industry brings in billions of dollars in sales each year, but it also emits large amounts of pollution. Of the total emissions of **greenhouse gases** in 2001, the pulp and

> **"The forestry industry is looking at ways to improve the sustainability of forest resources."**

paper industry was responsible for 15 per cent.

The forestry industry is looking at ways to improve the sustainability of forest

resources. Pulp and paper mills are also finding environmentally friendly and cost-effective ways of operating. Researchers such as Yonghao Ni are helping pulp and paper mills reach this goal.

Yonghao Ni is a researcher who studies and develops methods to improve paper production. In 1985, Ni received his Bachelor of Engineering Degree from the Northwest Institute of Light Industry in China. Ni then completed both his Masters and Ph.D. degrees in Chemical Engineering at McGill University in Montreal. Ni has been successful in reducing chemical waste at pulp and paper mills. In 2002, Ni was given a Canada Research Chair, a seven-year research position.

While a member of the Dr. Jack McKenzie Limerick Pulp and Paper Research and Education Centre, Ni created a method of bleaching paper that uses less peroxide and reduces waste. Ni called his new bleaching method the PM process. The PM process is now used in mills across North America.

■ Forestry scientists investigate new ways to process wood and examine forest growth and tree health.

Careers in Forestry

Today's forestry industry is about more than cutting down trees. People working in forestry have to be aware of the environmental issues their industry faces and be willing to strike a balance between the need for timber, the needs of the environment, and the social and cultural needs of the people who use the forest.

Forest Engineer

Duties: Plans and directs the construction, installation, and use of structures, equipment, and transportation networks concerned with the removal of timber from a forested area

Education: Bachelor degree in forestry or forestry technician certification

Interests: Computers, mapping, data management

Forest engineers handle the practical work of getting timber from the forest to the market. They survey and draw maps of the land in order to plan how to best use the area. Logging roads and railways are constructed in areas decided upon by forest engineers. The layout of a logging camp will also be organized by the forest engineer so that the placement of loading docks, bridges, cables, storage areas, and water and sewage systems allows for the efficient and safe removal of logs from the area. After planning the layout of the area and the transportation routes, the forest engineer also selects the methods and equipment to be used in making the plan a reality.

Forest engineers study the best ways to log a forest, including the infrastructure needed to transport felled trees to the market.

An industrial forester ensures that forests are properly managed and not over-logged.

Industrial Forester

Duties: Locating timber sources, negotiating the purchase of timber, and hiring workers to remove the trees from the location and send them to market

Education: Bachelor or master's degree in forestry

Interests: Science, mathematics, economics, computers

Industrial foresters work for companies that sell wood and wood products. They may manage the timber inventory of a company-owned forest or purchase timber from the owners of private forests. In order to properly manage the timber inventory, industrial foresters have to balance the economic needs of the industry with the impact the removal of trees has on the environment. Before removing the trees from an area of forest, industrial foresters determine the best way to conserve wildlife habitats, water quality, and soil conditions. They also make sure that laws regarding the environment are followed. Maintaining the sustainability of the forests is an integral part of the industrial forester's job.

Forestry Ecosystem Modeller

Duties: Analyzing information to support the sustainability of an area's forests

Education: Master's degree in forestry, ecology, or related biological science

Interests: Ecology, environmental issues, data management, computers

Model forests are working examples of sustainable forest management. Forestry ecosystem modellers develop ways to manage forests so that they remain healthy and productive even when being logged for their timber. Modellers create systems for the collection, storage, and retrieval of data about the condition of a forested area and the ways in which the forest is being used. This information is then analyzed to determine how forests can be managed more effectively and in a more sustainable fashion. From this analysis, forestry ecosystem modellers create new forest management techniques.

Model forests demonstrate responsible forest management.

Facing the Issues

Forests are an integral part of the global environment. By absorbing carbon dioxide and releasing oxygen, trees play an important role in controlling **global warming**. Forests are also rich in **biodiversity**. Many animals and plants reside in Canada's forests and rely on forest cover for their survival. Humans use the forests on a social level, for camping, hiking, and hunting, as well as other recreational activities. Finally, forests possess cultural significance to Canada's Aboriginal Peoples and are an important part of their spiritual heritage. These environmental, social, and cultural concerns must all be taken into consideration when forested land is used for business purposes.

> **Like humans, trees are also susceptible to diseases.**

Trees are cut down for a variety of reasons—to supply the forestry industry being the most obvious. Large tracts of Alberta's **boreal** forest are being removed to accommodate the growing oil and gas industry. As Canada develops into a more urban-populated country, forests are being removed to make way for expanding communities. The forestry industry is seen as part of a growing environmental problem that is resulting in the loss of Canada's forested land. People are looking to the industry to manage itself responsibly and in a way that promotes sustainability so that Canada always has forested land.

With limits on the amount of forest that can be harvested each year, it is important

Forest fires can start because of natural causes or be set and controlled by officials to promote new plant growth.

Many animals live in forests, such as deer, moose, elk, wolves, and birds.

to the forestry industry that the forests be healthy. Unfortunately, nature does not always cooperate with this goal. Forest fires are both helpful and harmful to the health of the forest and forestry industry. On the one hand, a forest fire can actually help regenerate forested areas that have lost trees due to the industry. On the other hand, fire also wipes out large areas of forest that the industry could use. Like humans, trees are also susceptible to diseases. Trees affected by disease do not provide quality wood or wood products and therefore cannot be used by the industry for this purpose. Insects can wreak havoc on trees as well. When allowed to spread, infestations can ruin large sections of forest, making the trees useless to the industry.

Canada's forestry industry also faces issues relating to international trade. Some countries put restrictions on imports of wood and wood products. These restrictions can involve product labelling requirements and quality standards. Before Canada can ship wood to these countries, it must make sure that all import conditions have been met. In some cases, countries put **quotas** on the amount of wood they will import.

Debate

Old growth forests are forests that have been able to grow for many years with little to no human interference. Only 20 percent of the world's old growth forests remain—mainly in Canada, Russia, and South America. The loss of these forests is at least partially due to the forestry industry. Should the forestry industry be allowed to log old growth forests?

YES Forests are able to regenerate after natural and human-induced disturbances. The trees will grow back.

The forestry industry contributes to Canada's economy. Logging these trees helps bring more money into the country.

Not every old growth tree is logged. Areas of forest are still set aside to house animals and protect water sources.

NO Cutting down trees destroys ecosystems that have taken years to develop. Many species of plants and animals will be lost.

Old growth forests have more value when allowed to stand. They bring in money through tourism and recreation.

Forests provide an environmental service. They provide water sources and reduce salinity in agricultural land.

Canadian Forestry in the World

Canada is home to 309 million hectares of forested land, most of which is boreal forest. Boreal forests are made up primarily of softwood trees. The viability of softwood as a product has led to a worldwide need.

In 2003, Canada produced 77.6 million cubic metres of softwood lumber. This amount ranked the country as the world's second largest producer of softwood lumber after the United States. Canada accounted for 14 percent of world production, while the United States produced 22 percent of the world's softwood lumber in that year.

Canada is the world's top-ranking producer of newsprint.

The United States also took the lead in worldwide production of wood pulp, with 28 percent of total production in 2003. Canada followed in second place, producing 14 percent of the world's wood pulp, or about 26 million tonnes. China ranked third, with 10 percent of world production. Sweden and Finland tied for the fourth-place ranking, with both producing six percent of the world's pulp production.

Certain types of plants can grow only in specific areas of Canada. Some areas, such as the Rocky Mountains, cannot support large plants. The point above which large plants, like trees, stop growing is called the tree line.

Wood pulp is used to make a variety of paper products, such as labels. In factories, the pulp is bleached and processed until it is ready to be used as paper.

Most wood pulp is used to make paper and paper products, and Canada has a number of pulp and paper mills that take the pulp through this process. The country is the world's top-ranking producer of newsprint, accounting for about 21 percent of total production. When combined with the production of other paper products, however, Canada's world ranking falls. In 2003, the country ranked fourth in the production of paper and paper products, tying with Germany. Both countries were responsible for six percent of the world's production. The United States was the top producer, making 25 percent of the world's

paper and paper products in that year. China and Japan ranked second and third, with 12 and nine percent respectively.

BUSINESS BITS

Canada has been the world's largest producer of newsprint for more than 50 years.

The forestry industry harvests approximately 750,000 hectares of Canada's boreal forest every year.

Russia, Brazil, and Canada are considered to be the "superpowers" of forest resources. While Brazil has the most rain forests, Russia and Canada both have large tracts of boreal forest.

Forests Around the World

Forests cover about 4 billion hectares, or 30 percent, of the world's total land area. Together, the Russian Federation, Brazil, Canada, the United States, and China possess more than half of this forested land. Not all forests are alike, however. The type of forest is often determined by its location. About 56 percent of the world's forests are considered to be tropical or subtropical, while 44 percent are either temperate or boreal. This map shows the boreal and temperate forest regions of the world.

THINK ABOUT IT ▼

Approximately 13 million hectares of the world's forests are lost every year. If this rate were to continue without interruption, how long would it take for the world's forests to disappear entirely?

Tropical Forests ☐

Temperate and Boreal Forests ☐

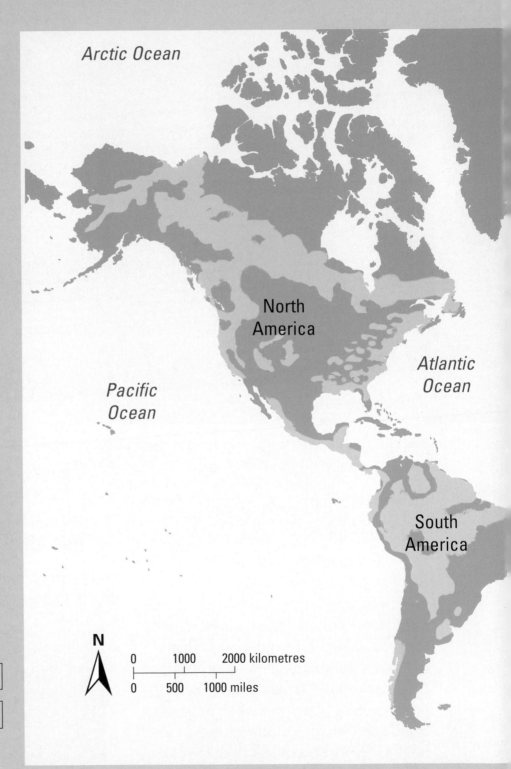

Arctic Ocean

North America

Pacific Ocean

Atlantic Ocean

South America

N

0   1000   2000 kilometres

0   500   1000 miles

Arctic Ocean

Asia

Europe

Africa

Pacific
Ocean

Atlantic
Ocean

Indian
Ocean

Australia

Charting the World's Forests

Distribution of Forest Cover

Forests are vital to the health of the planet. They play a critical role in moderating the world's climate, conserving soil, and providing habitat for wildlife.

(Percentage of the world's total forest cover)

Region	Percentage
Europe	27%
South America	23%
Africa	17%
Asia	14%
North and Central America	14%
Oceania	5%

The Big Ten

Ten countries hold two-thirds of the world's forests. Brazil alone harbours one-third of all tropical rain forest.

Forested area (million hectares)

Country	Million hectares
Indonesia	88
Dem. Rep. of Congo	134
Australia	164
China	197
United States	303
Canada	310
Brazil	478
Russian Federation	809
Peru	69
India	68

How Wood is Used

In developed countries, wood is used mainly for industrial purposes, with pulp and paper products taking on more importance. In the developing countries, most cut timber is used for fuel, either as firewood or charcoal.

Wood removal (2005) Million cubic metres

Africa	670
Asia	370
Europe	680
North and Central America	830
Oceania	70
South America	400

Designated Functions of Global Forests (2005)

Wood production continues to be the main function of many forests. In fact, 34 percent of the world's forests are used for the production of forest products.

Production	34.1%
Protection of soil and water	9.3%
Conservation of biodiversity	11.2%
Social services	3.7%
Multiple purpose	33.8%
Unknown function	7.8%

Supplying the Demand

The forestry industry profits from the sale of timber, lumber, wood pulp, and wood and paper products. These items are sold within Canada and to countries all over the world. The purchase of these products is based on supply and demand. Supply indicates the people or countries that have a product, while demand indicates the people or countries that need the product. There are many circumstances under which a country may need a product. It may not have enough forested land to support a forestry industry. It may have the forests but not the technology, knowledge, or human resources required to develop the industry.

The countries that can provide these products often have a surplus of the item. In the case of Canadian wood, Canada is able to harvest far more timber than it needs for its own use. Its extra forest products are sold to the countries that need them. When countries buy and sell products to each other, they are called trading partners. Trading involves importing and exporting products between countries. When a country imports a product, it brings the product into its country. When a country exports a product, it sends the product to another country.

Trade between countries is very dependent on prices. Countries needing forest products want to get what they need at a fair price. Canada is not the only country capable of supplying forest products. It needs to make sure that its prices are competitive in the international market. This means

Trade between countries is very dependent on prices.

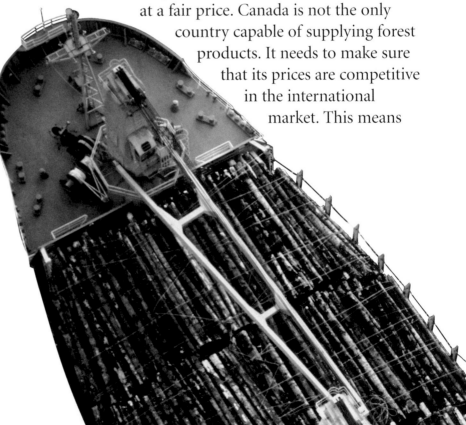

In 2005, Canada exported around 8.5 billion dollars' worth of lumber to the United States, most of which was softwood from British Columbia.

BUSINESS BITS

Exports of Canadian forest products account for about 79 percent of the country's total annual production.

Global trade in wood products totaled $150 billion (U.S.) in 2003.

Canadian forest products are exported to more than 100 countries around the world.

In order to remain competitive in the international lumber market, Canada must maintain healthy, sustainable forests. One way is to designate protected areas, such as Spray Valley Provincial Park in Alberta.

Trade in Canada's Forestry Sector

Year	Exports ($ billion)	Imports ($ billion)
1992	$24	$4
1993	$27	$5
1994	$32	$5.5
1995	$41	$6
1996	$39	$6
1997	$39	$7
1998	$40	$8.5
1999	$44	$9
2000	$48	$10
2001	$45	$9.5
2002	$43	$9.7
2003	$40	$9.5

that the people that set the prices must be aware of what price other countries are charging for the same product and how much of the product is needed in other countries. If the price is set too high and other countries are selling for less, the countries that need the product are more likely to buy it at the less expensive price. Likewise, if the product is not in demand, pricing it too high will limit the chances of selling it.

The quality of the product also affects its pricing. If the wood has been contaminated by disease or an insect infestation, for example, it will not get a good price on the market and may not even sell at all. Countries may then try to find healthier wood from other sources.

THINK ABOUT IT ▼

While Canada is known for its export of wood and wood products, it also imports these products into the country. Take a look at the chart above. How have Canada's imports of forest products compared to its exports over the years? Why is there such a big gap between the two?

From Canada to the World

Canada is the world's top exporter of forest products. In 2004, exports of Canadian forest products totalled $44.6 billion. Softwood lumber, wood pulp, and newsprint made up the majority of forest products exported. Wood panelling and other paper products also contributed to this total. Canada's main forest-product customers are the United States, the European Union, Japan, China, South America, and Central America.

Softwood lumber is by far the biggest forest-product export, accounting for approximately 25 percent, or $11 billion, of the exports.

Softwood lumber is by far the biggest forest-product export, accounting for approximately 25 percent, or $11 billion, of the exports. The United States is the major customer. It takes about 80 percent of Canada's softwood lumber exports, while Japan and the European Union import approximately 17 percent.

Wood pulp is Canada's second largest forest-product export, accounting for about 16 percent, or $7 billion, of Canada's export sales. The

Logs can be loaded onto trailers and carried by truck to sawmills and other locations.

THINK ABOUT IT ▼

Canada's forestry industry has had its share of ups and downs over the years, with export sales both peaking and plunging at different times. What factors affect the sales of forest products to other countries? Why might some years bring in more money than others?

Some companies make paper using mechanical wood pulp, made by grinding lumber with machines. More of the tree is used than with other methods, and less waste is produced.

United States is also Canada's top wood pulp customer, taking about 41 percent of the exports. The European Union imports approximately 23 percent of Canada's wood pulp exports, while China receives about 12 percent.

Newsprint made up about 12 percent, or $5 billion, of Canada's forest-product exports in 2004. Major customers of Canadian newsprint include the United States, the European Union, and India. Newsprint exports to the United States accounted for about 76 percent of all newsprint leaving Canada.

Forestry Exports

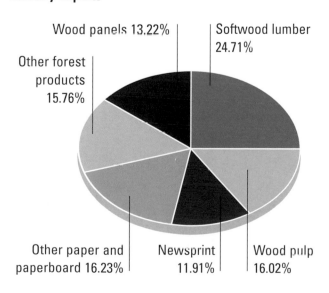

Wood panels 13.22% | Softwood lumber 24.71%
Other forest products 15.76%
Other paper and paperboard 16.23% | Newsprint 11.91% | Wood pulp 16.02%

Main Export Markets

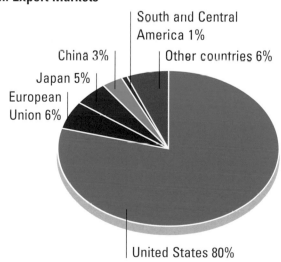

South and Central America 1%
China 3% | Other countries 6%
Japan 5%
European Union 6%
United States 80%

Due to rounding and other factors, totals may not add up to 100 percent.

Forestry Technology

Canada's forestry industry has benefited greatly from advances in science and technology. A forest's health and sustainability can be monitored and measured using **remote sensing** techniques, while **biotechnology** is being used to identify and generate trees of superior quality.

Due to the size and range of Canada's forested land, it is virtually impossible to keep track of changes taking place within the forest without the help of technology. Remote sensing techniques give forestry experts the information they need to properly assess and manage the challenges facing Canada's forests. Remote sensing covers a range of technologies and techniques. Each provides specialized forms of information that are invaluable to the forestry industry.

Aerial photography and satellites are perhaps the most well-known types of remote sensing. Satellites take pictures from space, while aerial photographs are taken from airplanes. The images taken by either

Genetic engineering has been used to increase the speed at which trees grow.

Satellite photographs show how the Amazon rain forest is quickly shrinking because of misuse.

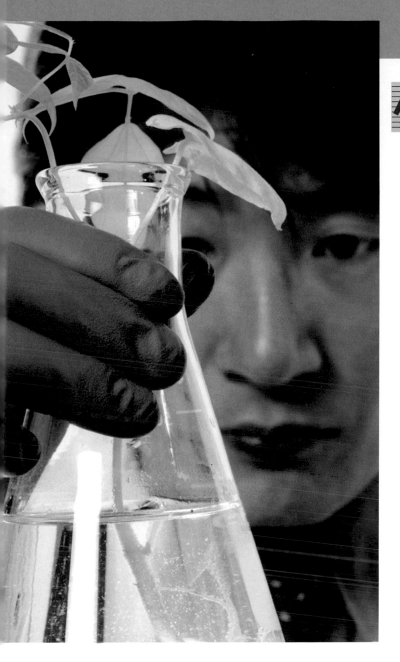

Genetic engineering could help sustain forests and improve lumber quality.

method help to keep track of the number of trees in the forests so that inventory levels stay stable enough to support the needs of the industry. They can also be used to measure the extent of damage caused by fire, and to make sure that there are enough trees available to support the business of forestry.

The health of the trees can also be assessed through the use of remote sensing imagery. The technology is so sophisticated that it can detect insect infestations. By knowing where and when an outbreak is occurring, scientists have a far better chance of keeping the infestation from spreading.

Biotechnology also helps keep trees healthy. In fact, the goal of biotechnology is to improve the quality of the trees in Canada's forests. Biotechnology research takes place in laboratories. There, research scientists perform various tests to determine how the **genetics** of various tree species differ and which tree types are stronger. They then use **genetic engineering** to improve the genetic structure of inferior trees. They do this by injecting genetic material from superior trees into the cells of other trees, thus transferring the superior traits of the donor tree. Genetic engineering has been used to increase the speed at which trees grow. This helps forests quickly replenish trees that have been logged so that the inventory available for the industry stays constant. Genetic engineering is also used to create trees that are more resistant to insect infestations.

Forestry's Impact on Canadians

Canada's forestry industry impacts on Canadians in a variety of ways. The industry helps Canada's economy with its export sales by bringing money into the country. It also provides many Canadians with jobs, either directly in the forestry industry or indirectly in jobs that support the industry. Many Canadians use forests for leisure pursuits, and the

> People are also affected by the impact the forestry industry has on the environment.

industry can be a potential threat to these activities. Aspects of the forestry industry also contribute to polluted air and water. This affects not only Canadians, but the world population also.

Approximately 361,000 people were employed in Canada's forestry industry in 2004, most working in the manufacturing end of the industry. However, the industry also provides jobs for people who do not work directly in forestry. The forestry industry relies on other businesses to help it create and ship products. Its pulp and paper mills require chemicals and packing materials. Logging requires

■ Canada's forests and other natural wonders are important to the Canadian tourism industry.

Canada's forests and national parks, including Yoho National Park, are important to the Canadian tourism industry.

specialized machinery. Trucks, trains, and ships are needed to get Canada's forest products where they have to go. All of these needs are supplied by businesses that have been set up to help the forestry industry. In 2004, these support businesses employed approximately 555,000 people whose jobs were specifically associated with forestry.

Forests provide Canadians with more than wood products. They serve as a place to escape to for relaxation and recreation. The animals and plants within them provide many Canadians with food and medicines.

People are also affected by the impact the forestry industry has on the environment. Cutting down trees limits Earth's ability to absorb carbon dioxide and generate oxygen. Chemicals used during the processing of wood and wood products are released into the air and nearby waters. Some of these chemicals have **toxic** properties that can cause damage to the environment. Many of these chemicals also release greenhouse gases into the air that contribute to the problem of global warming. Cutting down trees reduces Earth's ability to control its temperature, while greenhouse gas emissions encourage the global warming trend further.

BUSINESS BITS

Forest-oriented tourism brings in several billion dollars every year.

Canada has set aside 26.5 million hectares of forested land as national parks. Trees in these areas cannot be used by the forestry industry.

Helping Others

With 10 percent of the world's forests, Canada is a forest-rich country. Canada is also a large exporter of wood and paper products. Canada must carefully manage its forests to keep them healthy. Other countries look to Canada for help managing their forest resources. Of special interest to many of these countries is Canada's Model Forest Program.

The Model Forest Program was created in 1992 to address concerns about the environment and whether or not the forestry industry could be sustained.

There are now more than 40 model forests in the world, with Canada home to 11 of them.

Model forests rely on input from stakeholders, including governments, forestry companies, Aboriginal groups, and environmental agencies. The Model Forest Program tries to meet the needs of all the people who use forests.

The Canadian Model Forest Network started in 1992. The program showed promise early in its development, spurring the Canadian government to announce the international expansion of the Model Forest Network at the 1992 United Nations Conference on Environment and Development.

■ Good management of Canada's forests has commercial, recreational, and environmental benefits.

Three years later, the International Model Forest Network was created. Canada created this program and helps set up model forests in other parts of the world.

The Model Forest Network wants to maintain the health of the world's forests for future generations. Stakeholders' activities must support this goal. Each model forest has a formal governing structure so that rules are in place and are agreed to by all parties. Program members share their knowledge and experience to help preserve the economic and cultural value of model forests.

A model forest must have specific geographic features. It must be in an area with a diverse ecosystem that includes plant life, wildlife, and waterways. Humans must be present in the form of farms and towns. Industries, such as forestry, must also be included. The program studies ways that all these components together can work to sustain forests.

Members of the Canadian Model Forest Network travel the world to teach about model forests. As a result, the number of model forests has grown. There are now more than 40 model forests in the world.

The Gassinski Project

The McGregor Model Forest is working with a group of highly experienced Canadian, Russian, and international partners to improve market influences in the Russian Far East by establishing and supporting a number of commercially viable natural resource-based enterprises. The Gassinski Model Forest project, has been successful in broadening Canada's influence in the Far East, and in introducing technical assistance into its natural resource sector.

The project site is the Nanaiski Raion, of the Khabarovsk Krai region in the Russian Far East. The region is dominated by the forestry industry, but due to aggressive harvesting, the forest has been degraded. Instructors from Canadian post-secondary schools have visited the area to teach business classes and help with economic planning so that the forests can be sustainable for future generations.

The Gassinski project has been important to Khabarovsk Krai because it has provided an opportunity to develop long-term management plans for sustainable forestry in the area.

Source: McGregor Model Forest website

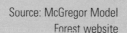

Looking to the Future

The future of the forestry industry in Canada is focussed on the issue of sustainability. Keeping forests healthy and viable for recreational users, Aboriginal groups, and the forestry industry requires a variety of approaches and techniques. Some may appear to be helping more than others. Whether through model forests or biotechnology, the goal is the same—to keep Canada's forests healthy and productive for future generations.

The growing popularity of the model forest program is a tribute to the commitment of forest stakeholders to sustainability. Cooperation among these stakeholders is helping to create understanding about the

Some of the biggest changes in practices have occurred in the pulp and paper industry.

various roles forests play in people's lives. With this understanding comes a willingness to work together so that informed decisions about forests can be made and applied. By expanding this concept on an international scale, more viewpoints about sustainability are being shared. This helps to assure the future of forests for people who rely on them, including forestry industry professionals.

Another way that sustainability is promoted is through certification programs. These programs are aimed primarily at the forestry industry. Certification programs set standards by which forests and forest products must be managed. The programs are set up to assess if the methods to manage a forest or create a wood product are environmentally

Canada's pulp and paper mills are looking for more efficient ways of producing pulp.

Biotechnology is applied to industries such as agriculture and forestry. Scientists look for ways to produce disease-resistant plants.

Science is taking forestry into the future in other ways as well. Through genetic engineering and other forms of biotechnology, scientists are recreating the tree. Trees that resist disease and ignore insects improve the health of the forest and keep it sustainable for the forestry industry as well as the other people that use it. Trees that are able to grow faster will allow the forest to regenerate itself more quickly after the area has been logged or had a forest fire. Forests are already known for their ability to regenerate. Biotechnology will improve upon this ability. The forestry industry, as well as the forest's other stakeholders, will benefit as a result.

friendly and promote sustainability. When a company meets these standards, it is given the right to advertise that it has done so. The sales of a company and its products can improve as a result of this recognition. Many forestry-related companies have adopted sustainable forestry practices because of certification programs.

Some of the biggest changes in practices have occurred in the pulp and paper industry. As one of the industry's major polluters, the pulp and paper industry has had to face much criticism over the years in regard to the dumping of chemicals into water and air. In response to this criticism, the industry has worked closely with scientists to discover new ways of processing wood and wood products with fewer chemicals, or at least chemicals that cause less harm to the environment. These efforts have been worthwhile. Since 1990, Canada's pulp and paper mills have been able to reduce their greenhouse gas emissions by 28 percent.

Insider Viewpoint

What does the future hold for Canadian forestry? Take a look at what people are saying.

"My vision is full of fear. …There's a lot of juggling of needs. …With our population growing, I see the point where there will be no forest resource left for people."

Lawrence Martin, Mayor of Cochrane, Ontario

"We need to manage the boreal forest better. …We need more natural cutblocks, and we need to minimize disturbances to the environment."

Jim Lopez, Executive Vice-President and President of the Forest Products Group, Tembec Inc

Timeline of Forestry Events

About 1,000 years ago

Forests cover about 60 million square kilometres of the planet.

2600 BC

Large-scale commercial logging operations are conducted in ancient Lebanon. The lumber is exported to Egypt and Sumeria.

AD 1621

Pilgrims in Massachusetts send a ship called *Fortune* back to England full of timber. The export of timber from the New World begins.

1899

Canada's federal forestry service begins with the appointment of Elihu Stewart as inspector of timber and forestry.

1900

The Canadian Forestry Association is established.

1907

The University of Toronto creates its Faculty of Forestry. It is Canada's oldest forestry faculty and is a pioneer in scientific forest management.

1930

The United States imposes a duty on imports of Canadian lumber.

1949

The Canada Forestry Act is passed.

1970

Brazilian rain forests remain an untouched natural resource.

1985

More than 200,000 sq km of Brazilian rain forest has been cut or destroyed.

1992

The first Canada Forest Accord signed by 29 government and non-government organizations, as well as hundreds of Canadians committed to the future of Canadian forests.

1992

Canada initiates its Model Forest Program to develop approaches to sustainable forest management.

1993

The Forest Stewardship Council (FSC) is founded.

1993

Half of the coastal forests of Clayoquot Sound on Vancouver Island are opened for logging.

1995

The World Commission on Forests and Sustainable Development (WCFSD) is set up.

1996

Canada and the United States sign the Softwood Lumber Agreement, a five-year trade agreement that sets quotas for the export of Canadian lumber into the United States.

1997

According to Greenpeace, international logging companies invest $100 million in the Amazon.

1997-1998

Fire destroys 20,000 sq km of forest in Brazil and a similar-sized area in Indonesia. Mexico and Central America also experience fires over very large areas.

1998

The United States and Canada experience an ice storm. In the United States alone, 20,000 sq km of forest are severely damaged, causing losses of more than $1 billion.

2000

The FAO's Global Forest Resources Assessment 2000, the most comprehensive survey of forest conditions, is released.

2001

About 900,000 sq km, or 2 percent, of global forest is certified under the Forest Stewardship Council.

2001

The Canada-United States Softwood Lumber Agreement lapses with no new agreement in place.

2003

The fifth National Forest Strategy (2003-2008), A Sustainable Forest: The Canadian Commitment is developed to provide direction for policy development, research initiatives, and activities to improve forestry practices.

2006

Canada and the United States make a new forest-product trade agreement.

Research Activity

The Logging Debate

The logging of Canada's forests has become a sensitive issue. The forestry industry sees economic opportunities in the forests. Others see logging as the reason for many environmental problems. In some parts of the country, public campaigns have been held to protest the logging of Canada's forested areas, especially old growth forests.

Both industry and environmental groups have persuasive arguments that justify their beliefs and actions. Further your understanding of these arguments by finding answers to these questions.

1. Why are forests logged?
2. What effect does logging have on wildlife, plant life, and the human population?
3. How does logging help the forest? How does it hinder the forest?
4. How does logging help and hinder the global environment?

Create a chart to illustrate the advantages and disadvantages of logging Canada's forests.

Forestry Experiment

Making Paper

For thousands of years, paper was made by hand. Egyptians made paper from an aquatic plant called papyrus. The Chinese beat down fishing nets and ropes to make paper. You can make your own paper using the instructions below.

Materials

used paper (newspaper, brown paper bag, wrapping paper)
bucket or pail
water
wooden spoon
plastic tub or tray (20 centimetres deep)
wire mesh (18 x 23 cm)
2 dish towels
sponge
plastic bag
books or other heavy objects

1. Tear up the paper and let it soak overnight in the bucket.
2. The next day, drain off the excess water.
3. Use the wooden spoon to mash the soaked paper into pulp.
4. Put equal amounts of water and pulp into the tub or tray. Mix together.
5. Slide the wire mesh sheet into the tub.
6. Lift the mesh out slowly and carefully as it will be covered with pulp.
7. Lay a dish towel on a flat surface.
8. Quickly place the mesh onto the cloth, with the pulp side down.
9. Press the mesh into the cloth with the sponge and squeeze out the excess water.
10. Peel the mesh from the cloth, leaving the pulp behind.
11. Put another dish towel on the pulp and press down firmly. If the paper becomes too thin, add more pulp.
12. Repeat these steps until all the pulp is pressed onto the cloth.
13. Place a plastic bag on top of the pulp and weigh it down with something heavy.
14. Leave the pulp for a few hours. Then gently peel the paper from the cloth. Leave the pieces on a flat surface and let them dry completely. You have now made paper.

What Do You Know?

M i X and Match

1)	Softwood tree	a)	forestry pioneer
2)	Canada Forest Accord	b)	genetic engineering
3)	National Forest Strategy	c)	model forest
4)	Dominion Forest Reserve Act	d)	logging machine
5)	biotechnology	e)	spruce
6)	remote sensing	f)	standards assessment
7)	skidder	g)	government agreement
8)	Gassinski Project	h)	satellites
9)	Yonghao Ni	i)	forest preservation program
10)	certification program	j)	forestry scientist
11)	Elihu Stewart	k)	government action plan

Answers:
1. e) 2. g) 3. k) 4. i) 5. b) 6. h) 7. d) 8. c) 9. j) 10. f) 11. a)

TRUE or FALSE?

1 Canada holds 20 percent of the world's forests.

2 In 2004, softwood lumber accounted for 25 percent of all exported forest products.

3 Lumber is a "second-stage" wood product.

4 Canada ranks second in the production of newsprint.

5 Trees in Canada's national parks cannot be used for logging.

Answers:
1. False 2. True 3. False 4. False 5. True.

MULTIPLE Choice

1 Which of the following is not a softwood tree?

a) pine

b) spruce

c) maple

d) fir

2 Which countries are called the "superpowers" of forest resources?

a) Russia, China, Canada

b) Russia, Canada, the United States

c) Brazil, Canada, China

d) Brazil, Canada, Russia

3 What is Canada's top forest-product export?

a) softwood lumber

b) newsprint

c) wood pulp

d) wood panelling

4 Which country is Canada's largest customer of forest products?

a) China

b) United States

c) Russia

d) European Union

5 Which sector of Canada's forestry industry employs the most people?

a) logging

b) manufacturing

c) transportation

d) forestry services

6 In what year was Canada's Model Forest Network launched?

a) 1988

b) 1990

c) 1992

d) 1994

Answers:
1. c 2. d 3. a
4. b 5. b 6. c

Further Research

Books

These books provide more information on forests and forestry in Canada.

Drushka, Ken. *Canada's Forests: A History.* Durham, NC: The Forest History Society, 2003.

Farrar, John L. *Trees in Canada.* Toronto: Fitzhenry & Whiteside Limited, 1995.

Parfitt, Ben. *Forest Follies: Adventures and Misadventures in the Great Canadian Forest.* British Columbia: Harbour Publishing, 1998.

Websites

To find out more about Canadian forestry, check out these websites.

Canadian Forest Service

www.nrcan.gc.ca/cfs/index_e.html

Canadian Institute of Forestry

www.cif-ifc.org

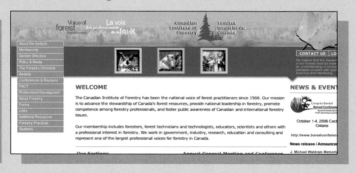

Canadian Forestry Association

www.canadianforestry.com

Glossary

biodiversity: a range of plant and animal life living within an environment

biotechnology: the use of microorganisms for beneficial effect

boreal: relating to the forested areas of the North

commercial: interested in financial return

conservation: protecting and maintaining the natural environment

cultural: relating to intellectual development or civilization

economy: a system of producing, distributing, and consuming goods and services

free trade agreement: an agreement made to remove tariffs and other barriers restricting the purchase and sale of goods between countries

genetic engineering: scientific change of the genetic structure of a living organism

genetics: the study of variation in plants and animals

global warming: an increase in the average temperature of Earth's atmosphere, enough to cause climate change

greenhouse gases: atmospheric gases that can reflect heat back to Earth

manufacturing: making something from raw materials

quotas: maximum quantities that can be created or shipped

remote sensing: gathering of information from a distance, using radar, aerial photography, and satellite imagery

softwood lumber: wood cut from trees such as spruce, fir, or pine

spirituality: concerned with sacred or religious things

stakeholders: people who have an interest in a business or enterprise

sustainable: capable of being maintained at a steady level without exhausting natural resources or causing severe ecological damage

tariffs: taxes

toxic: harmful or deadly

trade: the act of buying and selling goods and services

wood pulp: a moist mixture of tree fibres

Index

Aboriginal Peoples 6, 10, 15, 20, 36, 38
aerial photography 7, 32

biotechnology 32, 33, 38, 39, 44

Canada Forest Accord 11, 40, 44
certification 38, 39, 44
chemicals 16, 34, 35, 39

disease 7, 21,29, 39

economy 7, 21, 34, 37, 47
export 7, 14, 16, 28, 29, 30, 31, 34, 36, 40, 41, 45

forest fires 7, 20, 21, 39, 41
free trade 7

Gassinski Project 37, 44
global warming 20, 35

insects 7, 21, 29, 33, 39

logging 10, 12, 13, 18, 21, 34, 39, 40, 41, 42, 44, 45
lumber 6, 7, 8, 14, 15, 16 22, 28, 29, 30, 31, 33, 40, 41, 44, 45

model forest 7, 19, 36, 37, 38, 40, 44, 45

National Forest Strategy 11, 41, 44

old growth forests 21

pollution 16, 17, 34, 39
pulp and paper mills 5, 16, 17, 23, 34, 36, 38, 39

satellites 7, 32, 44
softwood lumber 6, 7, 14, 15, 22, 28, 30, 31, 41, 44, 45
Stewart, Elihu 11,40, 44
sustainability 7, 17, 19, 20, 32, 37, 38, 39, 40, 41

timber 7, 10, 11, 14, 18, 19, 27, 28, 40

wood pulp 6, 8, 16, 17, 22, 23, 28, 30, 31, 45